YOUR CLOSEST NEIGHBOR

The Husband's Handbook to Cultivating
Love and Forgiveness

JAMES A. LUSK, SR.

Publishing support provided by
Ignite Press
5070 N. Sixth St. #189
Fresno, CA 93710
www.IgnitePress.us

ISBN: 979-8-9892198-0-3
ISBN: 979-8-9892198-1-0 (E-book)

For bulk purchases and for booking, contact:

James A. Lusk, Sr.
jameslusk@your-closest-neighbor.com
Your-Closest-Neighbor.com

Library of Congress Control Number: 2023917011

Cover design by Nathaniel Dasco
Edited by Zoe Herald
Interior design by Jetlaunch

FIRST EDITION

Praise for *Your Closest Neighbor*

"Marriage must be one of the most complex of all human commitments. It buds with the promise of romance, friendship, unconditional love, unwavering loyalty, and unlimited sex. It's like a box that is filled with all the things you've ever wanted. When two people finally say 'I do', hopes and dreams are usually at their highest– a blank canvas, just waiting to be filled with color. What happens? In spite of all this, it doesn't take long before most couples realize that if it is a box, at its onset, it's an empty one. You can't take anything out of the box until you've put something in.

This is a book about putting things in. *In Your Closest Neighbor*, you're going to find a thoughtful and practical approach to putting things in. It describes what I would call real marriage. Written with reflective humility and courageous vulnerability, it tells a story about what marriage really is and what it takes to fill it with all the wonder you'd hoped for from the beginning."

Shane Ham, Senior Pastor Northpointe Community Church, Fresno, CA

"Are you the type of person who likes to learn from others through their experiences? In this book, Jim and Donna Lusk have openly shared their struggles in an effort to help others. They cover many of the skills we teach in our skills based program. It's so helpful when people are transparent about how they have been able to handle the challenges of marriage.

God's Word is what helped them navigate through the hard times. Jim's wife is his "car buddy" and my wife is my "serving others buddy". Read their story to find out who your buddy is."

Dave Belden, Executive Director
Healthy Marriage Coalition

To Donna, who has endured my shortcomings while dealing with her own struggles.

To our sons, Alan and Jeff, who have been there along the way even when times were tough. Thank you for still being willing to hang out with us.

Acknowledgments

Over the course of these years there are some people who need recognition in helping us work our way through our challenges.

First, I would like to thank God for giving me the words to write and the life to learn these truths. I truly feel that He led me through this process to teach me things that I had never considered and to share those with others.

I would also like to recognize Dr. Christopher Rosik for his work with Donna's depression and other diagnoses. And for his wisdom trickling down to me even when I didn't want it to. More recently, I would also like to thank Dr. Annie Fujikawa for her contributions to Donna's healing. She was an amazing resource at a time where it was needed.

There are so many others over the course of my life who have helped shape me into who I am. Pastors who have said the right things at the right time. Friends who have come alongside me at various times in my life. The encouragement, patience, and love they have given me cannot be measured. I am richly blessed by all the people who have been a part of my life.

TABLE OF CONTENTS

FOREWORD

I have known Jim Lusk for nearly 50 years, since we met in high school. I was actually closer to his brother and initially knew Jim as the pesky little brother, but we all grew up. I met Donna soon after Jim did and was pleased to attend their wedding in 1982. Being close to the family, we watched as their boys were born and as Donna began to deal with health issues. I knew that, if it were me, I would be greatly challenged to be facing what Jim was dealing with and he won my respect for staying the course. Obviously, you never know what goes on behind the curtain in another couple's marriage, but this book draws back that curtain to give the reader an up-close look at how Jim –and Donna– dealt with a long period of very challenging years.

    This book is not a whitewash job. It is a hard, introspective look at an imperfect man who was brave and humble enough to let God and wise counselors teach him –sometimes little by little– as he struggled with his situation, his marriage, and sometimes with his children. As you will find, Jim freely admits he often got it wrong. But he's getting it right a lot more often these days, with help from God and with Donna's faithful love, compassion, and forgiveness. This is a powerful story, packed with important truths for all men, particularly men who would like to not spend the next forty years learning this all the hard way.

Dave McGlasson
Former Director of Fresno/
Madera Youth for Christ

PREFACE

We all know that marriage is a challenge. We enter into marriage with our own set of ideas of what it will be like. For most of us, we had a lot to learn about living with somebody that we made a commitment to, somebody that we claimed to love.

What happens, then, when the day comes that we struggle to even like our spouse? How we deal with those days has a lot to do with how we view our marriage and how we view our spouse. It also affects and is affected by how we see God.

Donna is my wife of 40 years. We have two sons, Alan and Jeff. They are now in their late thirties with families of their own. While our struggles may not be typical, our reaction to them was. This is the story of 41 years together. It is the story of my struggles with her and myself and the things I learned when I finally listened to God.

One thing you will see that I particularly struggled with was in dealing with Donna's depression and mental illness. To say that I reacted badly would be an understatement, but with the grace of God and His gentle nudging I have learned and I am better at dealing with these things. I'm not there and likely will never get there fully.

Most of the verses I have addressed here are things that I have heard many times over the last 48 years without giving the words a second thought. That has made my life harder than it needed to be. I didn't give these words much thought until I decided to write about them. I thought I was a pretty good guy; I didn't beat my wife, I didn't berate her, *but* I didn't love her the way I was commanded to.

The chapters are arranged in an order that worked for us with forgiveness coming first. Our relationship with Jesus also started with Him forgiving us first. My hope through what I have written here is that you will find new ways to love your wife or husband and that you will be encouraged by our story. That there is hope in forgiveness.

I was asked once if I was writing a fiction or non-fiction book. Since I can be a bit of a smart aleck, I answered that for some it might be fiction, sadly...

CHAPTER 1
OUR STORY

Growing up was probably too easy for me. There was never much in the way of family drama, school was easy, and I grew up laid back with few cares. I have been described by classmates as happy go lucky. I have also been viewed as lazy by some because so much came so easily, but some things came so hard. I took very little in life seriously, so when I encountered serious things, I was absolutely unprepared. I had accepted Christ as my savior in 1974 when I was 14 and soon became involved in a church and youth group activities, especially the fun ones.

I met Donna at a Youth for Christ event in May 1981. That year I was a staff member on a local Campus Life club. Campus Life was YFC's high school ministry. It is unlikely that I would have been on staff that year if I had not broken my back a year earlier inner tubing in the snow with my church college group. The recovery made me impatient to get out and get a job so I had dropped out of college and had just finished a local trade school course in electronics at the end of April 1981. Had I not hurt myself, I might have gone away for school that year or made other choices.

Campus Life's annual mushball –I've also heard it referred to as "Chicago softball"– tournament was always a fun time. Most of the high school clubs had two teams, one of boys and one of girls. It was the major event at the end of the school year. Our team wasn't very good so we were out of the double-elimination tournament pretty early. My jacket was laying on the ground next to me as I was talking to a girl that I knew. All of a sudden there was ice landing on my jacket, having been tossed from behind me. I turned around and saw a girl that I did not know with a "Who? Me?" look (we've all seen that look...and given it...). The ice had come from a bucket with soft drinks in it that were for sale. After trying to get her playfully put into the ice bucket and not succeeding (this is actually a fairly important piece of what attracted me to her), we proceeded to start talking.

We found out that we had a lot of mutual friends. I also found out that she could spot a 1966 Plymouth Barracuda from two or three hundred yards away. When she tells the story, she says that is when she caught my attention. I would be dishonest if I didn't agree, at least to a point. I'm a car guy and was pretty proud of that car. Her being cute and a little feisty didn't hurt either.

Donna had been moved away from Fresno the summer before her senior year of high school in 1978, the year I graduated, and was back to find out about moving "home." That night, we went to the movies with her friend that she was staying with. To say that I was interested in her would be a gross understatement. There was something special there. I knew it right away, but Donna wouldn't know for a while. I did do something that was out of the ordinary for me. The next weekend I sent her flowers. This would be the source of some issues later on, which you will see. The flowers did get her attention, though.

Our relationship started out as a long distance one, with our first real date coming a month or so later. I had given her a choice, a day at the local amusement park or a picnic on the beach in Carmel. Carmel it was. We spent the whole day seeing the sights and getting to know each other. We drove 17-Mile Drive which we have done twice. The second time being our anniversary weekend in 2017. It may have been a good thing that my car radio died on the way to pick her up (kind of embarrassing for an electronics technician, though) so we had to talk. We wanted to spend more time together the next day, so I slept on her parent's couch that night.

During this time, we found out that we almost met four years earlier. Campus Life did a long weekend retreat every February for most of the high school groups. In 1977, that retreat was in Yosemite National Park. Turns out that we were both there. One of her good friends, Carla, was a girl that I knew from elementary school. Carla and I had been neighbors and friends, but we hadn't seen each other since she moved out of the neighborhood about six years earlier. My family moved out about a year later. I had spent quite a bit of time at that retreat catching up with Carla. When we weren't together, she and Donna were hanging out. We were apparently not meant to meet on that day.

Donna and I were married 50 weeks after we met, on May 1, 1982. Things were tough leading up to the wedding. I was laid off from my job two months prior and was spending time out of town looking for a new job. Donna showed signs of what I thought was stress when I would leave for a few days. She was very emotional each time. I thought this would get better after we got married and were in our own place. That didn't happen. Some days, she would get mad at me for going to work in the morning. I was a very confused 22-year-old.

My career has, primarily, been spent fixing electronic equipment and systems. Most of that has been doing field service, driving from site to site. I chose this type of work for many of the same reasons that I have chosen a lot of things, it's fun for me. There are challenges, but not very many. I recently finished my last actual job. I was building one-off manufacturing and test equipment. I found this to be very satisfying and fun as I was using my skills to build things.

As a technician I have been taught to look at cause and effect; To look at what part of a machine was last touched. With that in mind, I thought about the timing of the beginning of Donna's mood swings. The other thing that happened about the same time I lost my job is that she was put on the birth control pill. In 1982, there were whispered rumors of the pill causing mood swings. Nothing that was out in wide circulation, but the word was out there. Fortunately, Donna also has a very technical mind and when I laid out the timeline for her, she agreed that was the likely cause. I was relieved, but her doctor was not so enthusiastic about *our* diagnosis. He did, however, suggest a different, lower dose. Nope, no change.

We decided in January 1983 to do an experiment. Donna went off the pill and the wild emotions went away. Okay, we had proof, right? Nope, the doctor still didn't believe it. After trying a few different brands and dosages with no change in their effect we made a decision. By our first anniversary, I suggested that we just start our family.

We were told by some older Christians that the first year of marriage is tough and then it gets easy. Well, I have come to realize that two imperfect people living together is never really easy. Then add two little imperfect babies to the mix...

Our older son was born in February 1984, followed by another son two years later. During these years Donna had normal emotions, but I wasn't particularly happy. My job wasn't really satisfying and, as a dreamer, I always wondered if the grass was greener on the other side of the fence. Then, Donna started having problems with fatigue which, looking back on it, was likely depression and I am fairly certain that I contributed to it by not being fully present. There were other issues that aren't really relevant here, but suffice it to say that things were not very good for either of us.

In early 1988, Donna was given a new drug for what the doctor was calling chronic fatigue syndrome after multiple tests revealed nothing else. The drug? Prozac. For 18 months, things were back to normal. Donna had energy and was feeling pretty good. We were living in a nice little house and work was work. Then one day in 1989, as I describe it, she was dropped off a cliff. The cliff of suicidal depression. We would battle that for the next 27 years. For most of that time I battled against Donna rather than with her. Different drugs and different therapists were tried. We moved back to Fresno where I could have more help. That didn't really go as planned, but we tried. We bought our house in 1994 and we're still here and unlikely to ever move.

Over these years, I didn't want to deal with her depression and Donna knew it. We had some really rough spots, long ones. We didn't really talk about it, either. I didn't want to and Donna obliged even though she really needed my support. I also wasn't paying attention to God during those years. I still had my faith, but I didn't want to deal with God.

As a field service technician there is a lot of windshield time. That time between service calls that is generally used for daydreaming and thinking. Then one day around 2012, while I was particularly ready to throw in the towel, I heard this low, calm voice clearly say to me, "I made too much happen for you two to meet on that day and that time for you to throw it away." I was startled, but I knew what God meant and how many things had to happen for us both to be there at that Campus Life mushball tournament in 1981. That softened my heart a little to the point where I started to think of her instead of myself. Donna was still battling the depression, but I wasn't battling her nearly as much. We were better able to discuss her depression, but not as much as we really needed to

A couple of years later I had another revelation. Many people keep score. Donna is one of those people, but I tend not to. She thought that her negatives were so many that she could never get into the positive with me. The revelation? That the good times had so far outweighed the bad times that it wasn't even close. I started thinking about raising our sons, the friends we had made, going to car shows together, taking short trips, going shopping together, etc. Just doing life together got us through the tough times.

The lesson that I learned in these revelations is that we are called to forgive. I needed it from Donna at least as much as she needed it from me. I hadn't been there mentally when she needed me. I hadn't been the spiritual leader when I was called to be and I still struggle to be that.

That is the backstory to what I have learned over the last ten years or so and what has led me to write these words. It has been a process where God has taught me the things that have changed our marriage.

Thankfully, in January 2016, her depression was finally lifted when a doctor took her off of the anti-depressants, but not until after I had learned a few things. I am convinced that I needed to learn these things while Donna was still depressed. Otherwise, it would not have made the same impact. The truth of the matter is that I was wholly inadequate for the task that God had laid in front of me as her husband and I didn't look to Him for help; not for a long time. Next came the time to really learn.

The lessons started with a couple's study at church a few years ago on Gary Thomas' book, *Cherish*. During the first session, Gary recalls the story of a doctor friend of his. The young doctor was on rounds with an older doctor when they came into the room of an elderly patient who was being treated for a neuro-muscular disease. She was in a wheelchair and being cared for by her equally elderly husband, yet he was in much better shape than she was. She still lived at home with her husband.

The young doctor thought to himself that he never wanted to be in that position. The older doctor left the room, leaving the younger doctor in an awkward situation. The old man suddenly blurted out, "She's my fishing buddy, you know." He told the young doctor about all the places they fished over their 50-plus years of marriage. He beamed with pride as he recalled the stories.

When Gary finished telling this story I grabbed my wife's notes and wrote, "You're my car buddy." That was the first time I had seen her that way even though it should have been obvious. By that time, we had spent over 30 years building cars together, going to car shows together, chasing parts together, and, like the elderly couple in Gary's story, made memories and friends together. We have stories, both monumental and silly, but they are all part of the makeup of 40-plus years of marriage.

Our story also, eventually, had some similarities to the other couple. In 2017, Donna found herself in a wheelchair from degeneration and birth defects in both hips. I retired, in large part, to take care of her. Shortly after Donna was put in the wheelchair, we had to pack up our house for new flooring. As I was pushing her around Home Depot getting bins and boxes and stacking them in her lap in the chair, she made a comment that she couldn't see where we were going. I leaned in and whispered, "This is a lesson in trust." She says I also started pushing her a little faster. We both had a good laugh then and we still laugh about that to this day. In many ways I am still the same carefree guy that Donna married, but I have learned so much. So much that I never really wanted to know, but I am a better man for it. It really was a time of greater bonding for us. I am grateful for that time.

So, here we are five years after I retired. I did have to work some, for a while, but now I can pick whether or not I take a short term job for a little extra income. Donna has two new hips and no longer needs aids to walk. We still do life together. We even took a real vacation in November 2019 where, for the first time in our marriage, we went somewhere and stayed for a week. Typically, on a vacation we are not gone that long and we will go from place to place trying to see multiple locations in one trip, but this time we were gifted a week in Lake Havasu City by some friends as part of their timeshare. We were able to truly relax and enjoy each other. Many couples enter their retirement years not knowing their spouse and have a very tough time, but I'd encourage you to remember to forgive and remember what brought you together.

Donna and I are still building cars together, planning trips, seeing our grandkids, and basically working at living the life that God intended together. We are still not perfect in how we deal with each other, nor will we ever be. That's not the point. I will always need forgiveness and so will Donna. The point is that God is good.

CHAPTER 2
FORGIVENESS

Why forgive? Before we get into Scripture, we all need to acknowledge that none of us are perfect. We also know that, in our minds, we have an expectation on a certain level that our spouse will treat us perfectly. I can guarantee that just isn't going to happen. I have heard people state that if their spouse would just stop one behavior that all would be good, but the reality is that if they stopped one thing that bothered you another would come up. It's the nature of living so close to someone.

Romans 3:23 tells us, "...for all have sinned and fall short of the glory of God." That means you and your spouse. There's just no getting around this. Not only have we sinned against God, but we have sinned against those closest to us.

Mark 10:7-8 also puts marriage into the proper perspective,

> "7 'For this reason a man will leave his father and mother and be united to his wife,8 and the two will become one flesh.'
> So they are no longer two, but one flesh."

So, we take two imperfect souls and put them together as one. As we do this, you will do many things for which your spouse will need to forgive. The opposite is also true. Beginning to understand how these two truths affect our lives will begin to help you to live more peacefully with your spouse.

Matthew 6:14-15 can seem a little harsh,

> "14 For if you forgive other people when they sin against you, your heavenly Father will also forgive you. 15 But if you do not forgive others their sins, your Father will not forgive your sins."

We are called to forgive, but it is so hard with the person we live closest to. As we encounter things that we need to forgive, we will find out how we view the Word of God.

I have known for years the command that Jesus gave in Matthew 22:34-39:

> "34 Hearing that Jesus had silenced the Sadducees, the Pharisees got together. 35 One of them, an expert in the law, tested him with this question:36 'Teacher, which is the greatest commandment in the Law?'37 Jesus replied: 'Love the Lord your God with all your heart and with all

your soul and with all your mind.'[38] This
is the first and greatest commandment.
[39] And the second is like it: 'Love your
neighbor as yourself.'"

It was only in the last few years that I had a fresh
revelation. That is the answer to the question, "Who
is my closest neighbor?" The answer seems obvious,
but we tend not to live it or even think about it. My
closest neighbor is my wife. Second closest are my
children, parents, and brother.

But, you say, my spouse is so exasperating. How
many times should we forgive them? Jesus also
answered that question in Matthew 18:21-22:

"[21] Then Peter came to Jesus and asked,
'Lord, how many times shall I forgive my
brother or sister who sins against me? Up
to seven times?'"[22] Jesus answered, 'I tell
you, not seven times, but seventy times
seven times.'"

No, that doesn't mean that you get to count to
490 and stop. It means that you should be willing to
forgive more times than you can keep track of. We'll
talk about keeping score in Chapter 5.

The modern world has a lot of trouble with
Ephesians 5:22-24. These verses instruct wives to
submit to their husbands, but that command is
part of a larger command which I believe puts the
greater emphasis on how husbands should treat their
wives. More on that in Chapters 3 and 4. We should
start with verse 21 where we are all commanded to,
"Submit to one another out of reverence for Christ."
This is the servant attitude that we all should have.

Or, we could simply fashion our lives by following 1 Corinthians 13:

> "[4] Love is patient, love is kind. It does not envy, it does not boast, it is not proud. [5] It does not dishonor others, it is not self-seeking, it is not easily angered, it keeps no record of wrongs... [7] It always protects, always trusts, always hopes, always perseveres.[8]"

Love is patient. Ecclesiastes 7:8 provides a good basis for patience, "The end of a matter is better than its beginning, and patience is better than pride." Keeping our eye on the prize helps us to have enduring patience.

The end of 1 Corinthians 13:5 should be taken fully to heart. Love keeps no record of wrongs. The freedom you will feel when you let go of the hurts from your spouse not being perfect is beyond awesome. I found an interesting quote from, of all people, Marlene Dietrich, "Once a woman has forgiven her man, she must not reheat his sins for breakfast."

Proverbs 14:30 cautions us on the effects of envy, "A heart at peace gives life to the body, but envy rots the bones."

Pride is the subject of several Proverbs, most notably:

> 11:2 "When pride comes, then comes disgrace, but with humility comes wisdom."

> 13:10 "Where there is strife, there is pride, but wisdom is found in those who take advice."

16:18 "Pride goes before destruction, a haughty spirit before a fall."

I could go on, but pride is certainly a great hindrance to our lives and our ability to forgive others. It makes us think we are owed something.

Pulling 1 Corinthians 13:7 out to examine really shows where our hearts need to be, "It (love) always protects, always trusts, always hopes, always perseveres." How do we protect our spouse? By loving, forgiving, trusting, hoping, and persevering. It doesn't get any clearer in my mind than that. A slightly deeper dive into 1 Corinthians 13:4-8 will be found in Chapter 5.

Now, some are asking questions like, "What if my spouse is not showing me love, not trusting, not hoping, not forgiving?" This is where it will get difficult, but perhaps even more necessary. Go back to Colossians 3:13 as previously mentioned, "Bear with each other and forgive one another if any of you has a grievance against someone. Forgive as the Lord forgave you." There are no conditions here. Nobody is excluded from the command to forgive.

When these thoughts became clear to me, I already knew one thing about Donna. She blamed herself far more than me for any problems we had. I felt uncomfortable when comments were made about how good a man I was for staying with her through her depression. I knew that I had been wholly inadequate to give her the support that she needed and that I was commanded by God to give. I had finally changed, but knew that it had not been through my strength.

That's where Gary Thomas came back into the picture. He was at our church speaking for a couple's conference. I don't remember what Gary said, but on the way home I had another revelation that was as important as the first one. That is that, yes, I was wholly and completely inadequate to deal with the depression that Donna had been dealing with. I was also wholly and completely inadequate to deal with the normal things a woman goes through. It was shown to me in that moment that that was *the* point. Had any of that been through my strength, I would not have needed God to get me to the point where I could forgive Donna and to ask her to forgive me. But by God's strength, He got me there. God kept us together through all those years and here we are now with the blessings that God has given us in spite of our inadequacies.

To top it off, showing how good God had been to us, over the years I had not been asking Him to help because, quite frankly, there were times I wanted to throw in the towel. I had grown weary. I wanted to live for me. Each time Donna was suicidal, I was ready to walk away. There was one instance when our sons were teenagers that I did ask her to leave. She was at her parent's home for two weeks, but we decided to fight for our marriage even if my heart wasn't fully in it. We are here, together, because God wanted it and willed it. I am thankful that in the end His will prevailed over mine.

I cannot guarantee that your spouse will change if you adopt these attitudes in your heart, but I can practically guarantee that they won't if you do not. I can tell you this, Donna started changing as well because she saw changes in me. This is about being obedient to God and changing you, not some formula to change your spouse.

Forgiveness and Difficult Circumstances

We all took vows to "...love and to cherish, for better or worse, until death do us part," but this isn't real life for some. How does forgiveness fit into divorce? Are we really called to forgive an ex? I submit that the commands that God has given us do not change with the circumstance. Divorce does not give one freedom from the consequence of not forgiving one who has wronged us. That consequence is the development of bitterness and the alienation of loved ones. It prevents one from truly being able to love again.

I know someone who was married for 16 years to a man who was unfaithful. He died 32 years after the divorce. She was still so unforgiving that when he was dying, she told her daughters that she was glad he was going to die as he had wreaked havoc on a lot of lives. The hurt that her daughters felt was deep. Through everything and the flawed man that he was, he was their dad, they still loved him. Now, roughly 18 years later, the relationships are still strained. Think about how being unwilling to forgive will affect others.

Also, remember that while on the cross, Jesus forgave those who had put him there. In Luke 23 verse 34 Jesus says, "Father, forgive them, for they do not know what they are doing." They had not asked for it and didn't seem particularly inclined to think they needed it. Even during hard times with your spouse, consider how Christ treated those who had done wrong to Him without showing remorse.

Forgiveness also must become a way of life, not given just when you feel like it or when your spouse asks for it. It is an attitude to be cultivated and allowed to grow.

I would, however, caution anybody that is in an unsafe environment with abuse that none of this is a reason to stay where you are in danger, but you are still commanded to forgive. That means to forgive yourself and your spouse, even if you are going separate ways. Holding that spite inside will only destroy you further. The best remedy is creating a new life where you are completely free from the abuse.

CHAPTER 3
REST

Now that I have decided to make forgiveness a conscious effort and part of who I am, what's next? How do I make my life and marriage better? Let's look at Ephesians, chapter 5. This is yet another passage that I have heard many times over the course of my life. I finally got to the point where I wondered about it and what the words might mean.

Verses 25-28 will lead the way:

> "25 Husbands, love your wives, just as Christ loved the church and gave himself up for her 26 to make her holy, cleansing her by the washing with water through the word, 27 and to present her to himself as a radiant church, without stain or wrinkle or any other blemish, but holy and blameless. 28

In this same way, husbands ought to love their wives as their own bodies. He who loves his wife loves himself."

God asked me a question about this passage. That question was, "How did Christ love the church?" Seems obvious, but the answer changed my whole approach to my marriage. Christ loved and still loves the church by forgiving her first. That was difficult to wrap my arms around and was very convicting. Then, as my heart softened, it became clear how I was to treat my wife. He didn't forgive the church because they did anything to deserve it. He forgave because of His love. How many times have I heard the words of Christ and thought that I should treat my wife in that very same way?

I would also argue that wives should treat their husbands similarly.

Consider Ephesians 5:

> "[1] Follow God's example, therefore, as dearly loved children [2] and walk in the way of love, just as Christ loved us and gave himself up for us as a fragrant offering and sacrifice to God."

If I am to walk in the way of love following God's example, I need to look at His examples in His word. This command is to all Christians, regardless of sex or marital status. We are all to love as Christ loves.

Also, Philippians 2:

> "[1] Therefore if you have any encouragement from being united with Christ, if any comfort from his love, if any common

> sharing in the Spirit, if any tenderness and compassion, [2] then make my joy complete by being like-minded, having the same love, being one in spirit and of one mind. [3] Do nothing out of selfish ambition or vain conceit. Rather, in humility value others above yourselves, [4] not looking to your own interests but each of you to the interests of the others.
> [5] In your relationships with one another, have the same mindset as Christ Jesus..."

In all relationships I should work to have the same mindset as Christ. That is especially true in my relationship with Donna. We will not be like-minded in everything, but as far as forgiving each other we should be.

Finally, 1 John 2:

> "[6] Whoever claims to live in Him must live as Jesus did."

While I believe it begins with husbands loving their wives as Christ does the church, we are all called to be like Christ, whether we are husbands or wives or not married. We must strive to have the same mindset as Jesus and try to live as He did. So, what did Jesus have to say about His love?

"Give it a rest!"

Matthew 11:28 is a verse that I had heard many times, but in the context of how I love my wife the way Christ loves the church it has taken on a whole new meaning:

"Come to me, all who labor and are heavy laden, and I will give you rest."

Ponder on those words for a moment. Do I give my wife rest? Wives, do you give your husband rest?

But what does rest mean? Are there different kinds of rest? We Americans have a phrase often used in an attempt to end an argument, "Give it a rest." What is really meant by that is, "Give *me* some rest."

Donna and I came up with three types of rest: Physical, Emotional, and Spiritual. There may be more that you can think of, but these are our three. There are times when the rest you are giving your spouse is all three, but at times one or two will be excluded.

In the fall of 2018, Donna was getting around with a walker after physical therapy got her mostly out of the wheelchair. She still wasn't able to drive. I was substitute teaching, which meant I could take any day off that I wanted, but was still going to work most days. I knew that Donna was feeling home-bound. I took a Wednesday off and we drove to Kings Canyon National Park, which is not terribly far from our home. The trail to the General Grant tree is paved, but has several mild elevation changes. Donna was able to walk the entire path there and back with some stops to REST. Fortunately, her walker has a seat.

Getting out in God's beauty was an emotional and spiritual rest. Allowing Donna to get physical rest when she needed without becoming impatient was also important. Even more important was showing her that I was thinking about her and I knew what she needed. I could have asked her what she wanted to do or make excuses, but I needed to take charge of this. Often, if I ask her if she wants to do something she will say that she doesn't really need it or that we don't need to spend the money on her. I must ignore Donna's protestations and do the thing that will give her rest. She worries about spending money on her, even if the activity is something that I also want to do. As I work on understanding her needs, it becomes clearer what she needs at that moment. The more I act in this way the better she is at receiving it.

That was a very good day for so many reasons.

Over the course of this year, Donna has had many doctor appointments at Stanford. It is about a three hour drive each way. I don't mind the drive, but remember that I am also looking to have fun. A few weeks ago, I was thinking about an upcoming trip that would have us arriving at Stanford early in the morning after leaving home around 3a.m. Perfect, I thought. We needed to take a side trip. I had been to the Monterey Bay Aquarium when our younger son was 10 (he's 36 now). Donna had never been. So, I got tickets and we planned on taking Donna's Jazzy scooter as she still has a hard time with a long day on her feet and that kind of walking. The night before I discovered that the batteries were bad and it was too late to replace them. The aquarium does have wheelchairs so we figured we would just get one of theirs.

We spent five hours wandering around all of the exhibits and had a great time without Donna having to give up early due to fatigue. She also would not have been able to enjoy the day if she was running out of steam after an hour or so. We both needed a day like that as opposed to just another trip to Stanford and back. Donna needed the rest of the wheelchair and I needed to not have to worry about how long she could last. Donna could have been stubborn and insisted on walking, but that would not have given me emotional rest. Rest is not a mutually exclusive thing. We can both achieve rest in the same activity, but in some cases in different ways. When I stopped thinking about myself first, this was easy to see. When you think about giving your spouse rest, all of these things come into play.

How do you give rest?

Back to "Give it a rest." What are you arguing about? What are you blaming your spouse for? How do you give rest?

The Bible gives us instruction in this area as well. First for me is humility and we don't like humility. Most of us like to be the center of attention. We like to be praised. Humility opposes that.

Ephesians 4:2 is a start. Paul lays it out here that we need to be humble, gentle, and patient. The three go together in helping us to put others before ourselves:

> "Be completely humble and gentle; be patient, bearing with one another in love."

Colossians 3:12-14 is full of instructions for how to treat others, especially our spouse. This applies to all of us as Christians:

> "[12] Therefore, as God's chosen people, holy and dearly loved, clothe yourselves

> with compassion, kindness, humility, gentleness and patience. [13] Bear with each other and forgive one another if any of you has a grievance against someone. Forgive as the Lord forgave you. [14] And over all these virtues put on love, which binds them all together in perfect unity."

As I look for ways to show these virtues to Donna, it leads me to do things that I would not normally do. Compassion and kindness are found in considering her first. Humility is found in thinking less of myself.

I've never been big on buying flowers for Donna. They don't last very long and, well, it's just not *my* thing. See the selfishness overwhelming the last sentence. A couple of years ago I decided to buy some flowers for some occasion or for no occasion (I can't really remember). She was surprised and happy. I have done it a few more times since then. We talked about flowers not long ago and the thing is, it's not the flowers. How does your wife know that you're thinking about her when you aren't with her or even when you are? Flowers can give your wife rest because she knows where some of your thoughts have been. This is a form of emotional rest. However, some wives have been conditioned to see flowers as a peace offering after doing something wrong or as a bribe. This would not be emotional rest. That response will take more work. This is where knowing your spouse is critical and what behaviors will give her rest— and if you don't know, you should ask!

What does my emotional rest look like? Before your spouse can give you that rest you need to understand what that looks like to you. I like to tinker, not just on our old cars, but on other things. I taught myself how to weld. I'm not great at it, but I can melt metal and have it stay together most of the time. There are few things more satisfying than taking two pieces of metal and bonding them together. When I'm out in the garage, I am where I am at peace. Donna knows this and has no problem with me being out there and, at times, will come out to see my progress. You see, I don't have a "man cave." I have a space where she is welcome any time and she will occasionally lend a hand.

We're building a second two-car garage right now. Donna is as excited as I am about the progress. It is our garage to house her old car and mine. The car hobby is ours, not mine alone. This is very important, at least to us, that we do this together. It should never look like one of us is trying to get away from the other. That would be the opposite of rest. I have known couples that try to have their own space that the other really isn't welcome in. That's never really a good thing. Separating yourself from your spouse can lead to hurt feelings and the sense that there are things more important to you than they are.

Rest is also fleeting. It doesn't last just like a good night's sleep doesn't carry over to the next day, but a bad night's rest sure does. Rest needs to be something in your mind at all times. The thing about rest is that it is not lasting. For the same reason we need sleep every night we need to look at giving rest every day even if we gave rest the day before. In every moment, look for that opportunity. Think about little ways that you can give your spouse rest.

If you want to see a softening of their heart, show them constantly that you are thinking about them.

Donna is getting around better today, but she is still dealing with health problems. She can clean up the kitchen and does a better job than I do, but when I go in and do the dishes, she sees that I am doing something that is important to her.

We all recognize physical rest. Give your spouse time for a nap if they need one. Let them veg in front of the TV after work. I've known men who needed time to sit and read the newspaper after getting home from work, back when there was an afternoon paper. Maybe they need time to read a book to recover from the day. Whatever it is that gives your spouse physical rest, consider not making even a minor deal out of it.

Emotional rest is also wide and varied depending on your spouse, but it always involves showing him or her that you have them in your thoughts. Your spouse will find emotional rest in knowing that they are thought of and cared for, not just when you are with them. Knowing that you are thinking about them allows trust to be built and security in knowing that they are loved, wanted, and desired. Emotions will stay within a level of assuredness and not suspicion which brings unrest.

Exodus 33:

> "14 The Lord replied, 'My Presence will go with you, and I will give you rest.'"

Knowing of God's presence with His people would give them rest, an assuredness that they were not alone. This is a form of emotional and spiritual rest. Your spouse can also rest assured if they see that you are present, physically and emotionally.

Even God rested on the seventh day. If that isn't reason enough for you to give and to take rest, I don't know what would be. Genesis 2 describes how the heavens and earth were created:

> "[1] Thus the heavens and the earth were completed in all their vast array.
> [2] By the seventh day God had finished the work he had been doing; so on the seventh day he rested from all his work.
> [3] Then God blessed the seventh day and made it holy, because on it he rested from all the work of creating that he had done."

We spend too much time pursuing things and working too hard, but even God rested after working. What makes you think that you and your spouse don't need rest? We don't always have to be doing something.

Spiritual rest can be found in God's Word, but you don't have to be reading at that moment to find that rest. Take the time to reflect on the words throughout your day. As I have worked on this project, I have found things that should have been obvious, but I had never taken the time to contemplate their meaning and application. Giving myself space for spiritual rest is not easy for me. I tend to be one that needs to be actively "doing something", like building or fixing things. Allowing myself the time to just reflect on God and His word doesn't feel like "doing something" to me. I do try to reflect on these things while driving more now than in the past, though.

Spiritual rest is also found in praying, especially together for those things that are important and for thanking God for each other. I have given a great deal of thought to exactly what I am praying for in regards to Donna. She could use healing for her health problems, but I have realized that more important than that is that I pray for her to find God's peace, His spiritual rest.

Genesis 25:

> "²¹ Isaac prayed to the Lord on behalf of his wife…"

In this case Isaac was praying specifically for his wife to become pregnant, but it shows that he was looking to God for his and her needs and wants. The more we pray for our spouse the more we recognize their value to God and to ourselves.

Romans 12:

> "¹² Be joyful in hope, patient in affliction, faithful in prayer."

Being joyful in hope is having confidence that God holds the future. That joy does make it easier to be patient in affliction. All of this is possible if we are faithful in prayer. Our problems don't go away, as much as we would like them to, but as we look to God and pray for joy and patience we can find His rest.

1 Corinthians 7:

> "⁵ Do not deprive each other except perhaps by mutual consent and for a time, so that you may devote yourselves to prayer. Then come together again so that Satan

will not tempt you because of your lack of self-control."

As you separate yourselves to pray, pray for your spouse to find joy and peace. Pray for them to know their worth in God's eyes. Pray the same for yourself.
1 Peter 3:

> "7 Husbands, in the same way be considerate as you live with your wives, and treat them with respect as the weaker partner and as heirs with you of the gracious gift of life, so that nothing will hinder your prayers."

Prayer with and for your wife will bring spiritual peace. I have struggled with this for a very long time. It is uncomfortable for reasons I don't fully understand, but if I waited until I had it all together, I'd never get any of this written. I'm working on my prayer life. I have been contemplating a question over the last year or so, and that is, "What am I praying for?" When people ask you if you have any prayer requests, there is a sense that they are asking about health or external things. The more I think about this question the more I consider Paul's greetings and closings in the epistles. They are about grace, peace, and love.

As I pray for Donna, I consider what God would most like to see. I do pray for her health and for our years to come together, but I pray more for her to find peace in God's rest. We will all suffer health setbacks, especially as we age, but if we have found God's peace we will be sustained.

As you can see, rest is as important in my mind as is forgiveness. Talk about what rest looks like with your spouse and practice giving it. Also, practice receiving it. If you are weary, you need rest.

CHAPTER 4
LOVING LIKE JESUS

Servanthood

Another way Jesus shows how He loves the church and how we are supposed to love our wives can be found in Mark 10:43-45:

> "[43] Not so with you. Instead, whoever wants to become great among you must be your servant, [44] and whoever wants to be first must be slave of all. [45] For even the Son of Man did not come to be served, but to serve..."

Jesus was a leader of men, but in leading them He was serving them in so many ways even though His knowledge and skills were above theirs. As a field technician, my job was to serve the needs of others. I had skills that they did not possess, but rather than act superior, I was to put their needs above mine. In the same way as a husband, I need to look for ways to serve my wife.

At the last supper, Jesus washed the disciples' feet. They didn't have a good understanding as to why, even though He had explained that He had come to serve. This was a task normally reserved for lowly servants. John 13 captures Jesus's response:

> "[12] When he had finished washing their feet, he put on his clothes and returned to his place. 'Do you understand what I have done for you?' he asked them. [13] 'You call me 'Teacher' and 'Lord,' and rightly so, for that is what I am. [14] Now that I, your Lord and Teacher, have washed your feet, you also should wash one another's feet. [15] I have set you an example that you should do as I have done for you. [16] Very truly I tell you, no servant is greater than his master, nor is a messenger greater than the one who sent him. [17] Now that you know these things, you will be blessed if you do them.'"

Jesus showed how servanthood is something to strive for. There is a meme that I have seen online that states that the person posting it respects the janitor as much as the CEO. I have a completely different thought on the subject. I respect the janitor considerably more than the CEO. Why? The janitor does things that I do not want to do. He serves others by cleaning. While I may respect the CEO for the things he has accomplished, my respect for the janitor is for the things he does.

Donna has taken it upon herself to specifically thank servers for the job that they do when we are out to eat. Once when we were out, she went over to a table that was being bussed and thanked the bus boy for his work. As we think about those who serve us, we become more humble and grow in the desire to serve others.

This followed the disciples arguing about who among them was the greatest. Luke 22:

> "24 A dispute also arose among them as to which of them was considered to be greatest. 25 Jesus said to them, 'The kings of the Gentiles lord it over them; and those who exercise authority over them call themselves Benefactors. 26 But you are not to be like that. Instead, the greatest among you should be like the youngest, and the one who rules like the one who serves. 27 For who is greater, the one who is at the table or the one who serves? Is it not the one who is at the table? But I am among you as one who serves.'"

My son, Jeff, transferred high schools after his sophomore year. He showed up to the first baseball practice and met his new teammates, including the "star" of the team. There were several really good players, but Mike was the best. You will never meet a more humble and gracious high school player with great skill. In a place where fragile egos can show themselves, there was none. Mike greeted his new teammate without regard to who was greater. Jeff was just another guy to play ball with. They shared their knowledge with each other to make everyone better. When we stop trying to be first, we elevate all of those around us, especially at home.

Regarding myself as least puts me in the mindset of a servant. As I serve Donna with her physical limits, I find joy. There would be no joy if I demanded to be first. When I let her serve me, I am humbled.

Back to John 13:

> "⁶ He came to Simon Peter, who said to him, 'Lord, are you going to wash my feet?'
>
> ⁷ Jesus replied, 'You do not realize now what I am doing, but later you will understand.'
>
> ⁸ 'No,' said Peter, 'you shall never wash my feet.'
>
> Jesus answered, 'Unless I wash you, you have no part with me.'"

I have come to realize that there are times when Donna is serving me, I become uncomfortable. We do have a need to be like Peter. Serving others feeds our ego while being served humbles us, but marriage is about mutual service. At least now I recognize this within myself and I'm working on it.

I have a tendency to think that I can do things without help. Not long ago, I was in the process of building a new gate for the north side of our home. I had a steel frame on a table that I was painting. I could have managed to flip it over without help, but it was so much easier if I let Donna help me. She hadn't been feeling well, but allowing her to help made her feel more a part of the process. Truth be told, this whole project would not have happened without her help. About fifteen years ago, I was out in the side yard trying to figure out how to fit a second garage and RV parking into the existing space. My mind was set on a detached garage and nothing was fitting. She came out to see what I was doing. Normally, she can't visualize something that isn't there, but she simply asked why I didn't just attach the garage to the house. In that moment, it all fit in my mind. That was service of a different kind, but most welcome because my mind was set on something that couldn't be done.

Are we serving our spouse or are we trying to be above them? Do we demand that they do for us instead of us looking for ways to serve them? And, what does that look like? Over the last few months, we have battled flu and Covid (the flu was worse). Donna wanted some chicken noodle soup. We have found that Denny's has some of the best. It's not a long trip, but it does require going out to pick it up. And, no, I'm not using a delivery service for a $6 bowl of soup. This is such a simple form of service, but so meaningful.

While we should never demand to be served, we should humble ourselves and accept being served. All while striving to serve each other. Serving each other is another area of life where keeping score has become commonplace. If you have to remind your spouse of something you did in the past to serve them, then you probably are not serving them now. One other caution here is to not make this a competition where you try to outdo your spouse. Being served clashes with our sense of not being self-seeking while serving can boost our ego. Serving can cause us to say, "Look at me. Look at what I have done." If humility is not a quality you find in serving your spouse, you will find it a chore.

When our older son was a baby, Donna and I experienced an imbalance in serving each other; she was serving me too much and I was serving her too little. He wasn't sleeping through the night so she continually got up with him. Her reasoning was that I had to go to work in the morning. That was acceptable for me until one day I came home from work with her completely pale and throwing up. I took her to the urgent care at our medical center. They immediately took her into the back and within minutes sent her to the hospital. Her servanthood to me had drained her of so much that she needed to spend a few days resting (there's THAT word again) in the hospital. At the time I wasn't looking to be enough of a servant. Had we both had a servant's heart, she would not have become as sick.

I had Donna write about her views on servant-hood and how I had succeeded or not in the past few years. These are her words:

> "As a Christian we are, with God working in our hearts, becoming more Christ-like. Jesus was a servant to people. Being a servant to our spouse is very important. I can honestly say that Jim and I were not always doing things for each other totally out of a servant's heart. Part of being a

servant is our attitude in which we serve and receive being served. We are both learning to receive better, however, it is still uncomfortable at times.

Some of the ways Jim has served me over the years of our marriage have changed, from when our kids were little, to teenagers, to empty nesters, to health problems, to 40 years of being together. Serving a spouse is helping them, but not with the idea that it is an obligation; but with a sincerity of loving them and a desire to help.

With my many health issues now, Jim's serving me has increased 10-fold. At one time, a few years ago I was in a wheelchair and was having seizures. Not being allowed to drive because of the seizures was difficult. Full reliance on Jim on my part was an adjustment. Cooking, cleaning the house, laundry, and driving me to my appointments was now on Jim's shoulders. He stepped up and served me well for 2 years.

I had to learn to relinquish my control of how I wanted my house cleaned and allow Jim to clean in his way. At least it was being cleaned. After two years, I had received new hips and found out medication had been causing the seizures. Now, I was ready to be independent again. I was anxious to clean the house my way again. I found myself tiring easily so I am learning to accept Jim's help in still serving me. I also began in small ways to serve Jim. Some of that was to allow him to rest (there's that word again... –Jim) and watch what he wanted on TV. I didn't do it out of obligation and neither did Jim.

I could tell you, especially when I was in the wheelchair, that he was helping me out of his love for me and being obedient to what God was teaching him about servanthood and becoming more like Christ.

I found myself wanting to serve Jim now with a deeper love, in part, because of how he treated me during a very vulnerable time. I now have other health issues where Jim now serves me by driving hours to specialist doctor visits. Making sure that I'm okay when walking and stopping for me to rest. Walking slower when it hurts him (my hips hurt if I walk too slowly –Jim), but helps me. He still fixes dinner and brings it to me every night, pays the bills, and will help me vacuum if I ask. Allowing myself to serve, but to also accept Jim serving me has helped us both love each other at a deeper level.

Allow God to make the changes in your heart and mind to be more Christ-like. It is not easy or fun at times, but when you experience and see the love from the changes, it is worth it. I praise God for our 40 years of marriage and look forward to many more as we continue to serve each other."

How We Think

If we are to love our wives as Christ loves the church, what are we to think of her? Wives, what are you to think of your husbands? I will begin here with the truth that we all lack something. We really all lack a lot of things. With that in mind, consider how much we lack in our own ability to please God.

Jeremiah 29 includes a letter that the prophet Jeremiah sent from Jerusalem to those in exile that Nebuchadnezzar had taken to Babylon.

From that letter, Jeremiah 29:

> "[11] 'For I know the plans I have for you,' declares the Lord, 'plans to prosper you and not to harm you, plans to give you hope and a future.'"

While this was addressing those exiled at the time, we know that God has plans and is thinking about us, giving us hope and a future. Ask yourself if you have hope and plans for a future with your spouse. It is common in the workplace for a manager to ask where an employee sees themselves in five or ten years, but this question also needs to be asked in our personal lives. I have just finished a second garage at our home and have plans to finish restoring our two old cars in the next couple of years. These projects are so that we can both enjoy ourselves at car shows and just out driving with the top down and the wind blowing through what little hair I have left. Donna and I are also making plans for the next several years. We have travel plans, even plans to impact marriages through the things that I have learned the hard way.

Psalm 139:17 gives some insight into how God thinks of us:

> "How precious to me are your thoughts,
> God! How vast is the sum of them!"

God's thoughts of us are vast *and* precious. We need to think more of our wives (and husbands) in this sense. What would she think of your thoughts of her? We can cultivate the right kind of thoughts even when things are tough. When I realized that we had so many more good times than bad, it helped change my thoughts about Donna. I started thinking more about the good times. Even today we drove by a place we stayed at a few years ago for our anniversary and that started a discussion about another place we had stayed while on a vacation and a good meal we had. Remember the good and your thoughts will go to the good.

We talk about things we remember. One of our favorite stories happened the first year we were married. Remember times were tough and I was confused, but one day I stopped at a liquor store for a soft drink between service calls. On the counter by the register was a small display of squirt guns. I just knew that I had to have one. I got home that evening and Donna was at our kitchen sink with her back to me. I had filled the squirt gun up downstairs and unloaded it on her back. She laughed, but then insisted that she also needed one. I tried to explain that she didn't, but I lost that argument. After we got her a matching water pistol, we proceeded to have a squirt gun fight in the apartment for about an hour. Then we both grabbed towels and dried everything off. Two things made that night so memorable. First is that Donna knew that while I was struggling with her struggles, I had thought about her during the day. The other is that it took an edge off the struggle, even if only for a moment:

> "[29] Are not two sparrows sold for a penny? Yet not one of them will fall to the ground outside your Father's care. [30] And even the very hairs of your head are all numbered. [31] So don't be afraid; you are worth more than many sparrows" (Matthew 10).

Is your spouse worth more to you than two sparrows? How about more than that new fishing pole or classic car or anything else that you place value on. That doesn't mean to forsake all other things that you value, but your spouse should be more valuable to you than that. As I recognize Donna's needs more, I can react to them. When we took the trip to Kings Canyon on a day that I could have worked, it showed Donna that she was more valuable to me than a few dollars.

Understand that what God thinks of us has nothing to do with what we did or didn't do. The same should hold true for our spouse. We won't be as perfect with it, but when your wife does something that you don't like it is even more important to do things that show we are thinking about them, such as a last-minute trip to a place of beauty or out to dinner at a place that she really likes. Even the squirt gun fight was showing Donna that I was thinking about her while I was working. Wives, consider how your mood will change if you follow these ideas when your husband does something that hurts you. And, yes, this is one of the hardest things to do. It may be easy to "serve" your spouse when you are mad because you are making yourself out to be the "better," but your thoughts? Giving our thoughts to God in this way, that's a whole different thing.

Galatians 5:

> "[22] But the fruit of the Spirit is love, joy, peace, forbearance, kindness, goodness, faithfulness, [23] gentleness and self-control. Against such things there is no law."

As you find true, actionable love, the other fruits will follow. God, through the word written by Paul, must view these traits as valuable. What are you doing to get there? What am I doing to get there?

So, plan something for your spouse. Get a small token for them. Show them that they are in your thoughts daily. Our trip to Kings Canyon in 2018 was an example of this type of thinking. Did I want to go? Absolutely. But Donna needed to go and I knew it. When you tap into how your spouse thinks and learn to recognize their needs you will find that stress is reduced a great deal.

Friendship

Not only is Jesus King and Lord, he is our friend. He loves us as friends and we should love our spouse in the same way. Jesus shows His friendship in His own words, even calling his disciples friends multiple times (see Luke 5:34).

Jesus also speaks about friendship in John 15:13, arguing that, "Greater love has no one than this: to lay down one's life for one's friends." John 3:16 follows the theme of self-sacrifice in friendship, saying, "For God so loved the world that he gave his one and only Son, that whoever believes in him shall not perish but have eternal life."

While we are unlikely in this day and age to be asked to lay down our physical life for our spouse, we are to lay down our selfish desires for her. But, what does that look like? Donna has been living with certain dietary restrictions for the last couple of years. It makes restaurant selection difficult at times, especially when I am looking to try something new and different. I try to make sure that there are good choices for her to eat, but will also go to two places for take-out so that we both can get what we want and can eat.

The more you think about your spouse as your friend, the more you will look for ways to treat them as a friend. Proverbs 17:17 states, "A friend loves at all times…" while Song of Songs 5:16 tells of the feelings a woman has for her husband, "His mouth is sweetness itself; he is altogether lovely. This is my beloved, this is my friend, daughters of Jerusalem."

As I see Donna as my friend I want to include her in all parts of my life.

Donna and I have talked about the roughest times in our marriage and what kept us together. It was friendship. We still did all sorts of things together, whether that was just going to the store or going on a trip somewhere. We did things that friends do.

John 15:

> "[15] I no longer call you servants, because a servant does not know his master's business. Instead, I have called you friends, for everything that I learned from my Father I have made known to you."

Jesus made this statement to His disciples after they had abandoned Him on the cross. We need to view our spouse as a friend even, perhaps especially, after they have done something that hurts us. Many times the disciples disappointed Jesus with their unbelief and their actions, but he never gave up on any of them. Even after Judas Iscariot betrayed Him, Jesus did not condemn him. Jesus was a friend to the end as we should be. When Peter claimed three times to have not known Jesus, he was forgiven. Jesus didn't even tell him, "I told you so."

Friends have fun together (remember Donna is my car buddy), but also do mundane things together, and sometimes they do hard things together. Friends include each other in their lives. Think back to your best friend growing up. They were the first person you wanted to tell about something good that happened and the first person you went to when something bad happened. Donna is that person for me. Going through Donna's depression was hard and we didn't always do it together. Raising children was also hard at times, but we did do that together.

Cultivate your friendship with your spouse in the same way Jesus cultivates you as a friend. Include them in your plans. For many reasons I make most of our plans, but I want Donna there because as well as being my wife she is my friend.

Grace and Mercy

God, through Jesus, loves us by showing humanity grace and mercy. What do these words mean? How should we apply them to loving our spouse the way Christ loves the church?

Grace is a favor from God that is not earned. This is not dependent on anything we have done.

Mercy is the compassion or forgiveness given to one whom you have the power to punish or harm.

Within the marriage relationship we all have the power to punish or harm. Given that we will never be perfect in how we treat our spouse the world thinks it is fine to punish for the wrong our spouse has done, but as we have been commanded to be more Christ-like we must consider another approach.

That approach is grace through forgiveness. Romans 3:24 states this so simply that, "...all are justified freely by his grace through the redemption that came by Christ Jesus." The pure definition of God's grace is found in Romans 11:6, which says, "And if by grace, then it cannot be based on works; if it were, grace would no longer be grace."

Paul also demonstrates how he views grace given freely to the churches in his epistles in both the greeting and in the post-script. Most start and end with a variation of 1 Corinthians 1:3: "Grace and peace to you from God our Father and the Lord Jesus Christ."

How much more would our spouse feel the peace of God if we were to work this attitude into our speech and action? As you think more about extending grace, peace should follow.

In the Sermon on the Mount, Jesus begins with what is known as the Beatitudes. In Matthew 5:7 Jesus talks about mercy:

> "Blessed are the merciful,
> for they will be shown mercy."

Such a simple statement, but oh so true. Both in the context of our relationship with Christ, but in our earthly relationships, as well. However, treating your spouse with mercy and grace will not necessarily get grace and mercy back from them. Ours or their sinful nature may get in the way, but if you do not show mercy and grace I can practically guarantee that you will not receive them in return.

How We Talk

How do we talk to our spouse? Are we critical? Do we build up? Words have the power to destroy or to uplift. What words do you use when your spouse inevitably does something that you disagree with or think is wrong? Bear in mind that you may be right, but this is where you have a choice to be Christ-like or not.

Romans 15:2 states:

> "Each of us should please our neighbors for their good, to build them up."

While 1 Corinthians 8:1 puts it even more simply:

> "...while love builds up."

In Ephesians 4:29 Paul makes it even more clear how we are to talk to others, especially our spouse:

> "Do not let any unwholesome talk come out of your mouths, but only what is helpful for building others up according to their needs, that it may benefit those who listen."

And, again in 1 Thessalonians 5:11:

> "Therefore encourage one another and build each other up, just as in fact you are doing."

Our words can build up and they can destroy. This is where each marriage is different. In one relationship, certain words won't hurt whereas in others the same words can destroy. This is where knowing your spouse is absolutely necessary. Due to Donna's mental illness, I have had to learn things that trigger her. We have talked about them and I try to avoid saying them, but there are times I will hear those words from somebody else and I know where her mind will go and that we will need to have a gentle conversation about those things. I cannot tell her to not allow those words to trigger her. I don't get to decide those things. As I understand more about Donna's struggles in this area, I can tell when something will trigger her before we talk about it. Often, I cringe inside when people say these things, but my goal is to talk about them and give Donna a different perspective into what was said or just explain that others can be insensitive and often wrong when there is no other way to look at it.

Faithfulness

What is faithfulness?

Merriam-Webster defines faithful as steadfast in affection or allegiance, firm in adherence to promises, and given with strong assurance (there are others, but these are the definitions that apply here).

What does God have to say about His faithfulness? What does that mean for us?

Joshua 1:5b shows God's faithfulness to us:

> "As I was with Moses, so I will be with you;
> I will never leave you nor forsake you."

What does that look like in marriage? Leaving has an obvious meaning, physically leaving. We should be committed to never leaving even when things get tough unless your situation is abusive and dangerous.

Forsake has a similar meaning to leaving, but –in my opinion– is much stronger. Forsaken means abandoning or deserting. As God loves, so should we. Here is where things get into our thoughts. Whereas I see leaving is physical, forsaking is mental. You don't have to walk out the door to abandon someone. Separation mentally can be harder on someone than separation physically. It can also be more subtle.

As you are walking through life with your spouse, if you are looking for a way out you have already forsaken them. Your thoughts and feelings are not there and your spouse will know it. As I struggled with Donna's depression, I deserted her in so many ways. She knew it and it took God to remind me of His faithfulness to change my thoughts toward her.

Just changing my thoughts was not enough, however. The change in my thoughts needed to result in a change in my behavior. I needed to be steadfast with her, letting her know in words and deeds that I was not going anywhere. This came up again recently as her thyroid hormone levels were way off, which makes her suicidal. During these tough times, I make sure that she sees me stand by her side. One of the ways that I have done this is to take the stress of driving off her by taking her to her appointments. This takes time and consistency.

1 Corinthians 4:2 says, "Now it is required that those who have been given a trust must prove faithful." In no small way has God given us our spouse as a trust. We are to see that God has trusted us with a son or daughter and take that trust seriously.

As I thought about never leaving or forsaking, I thought about the older couple in Gary Thomas' story in chapter one. I also thought about Donna and the fact that our car hobby is not only mine, it is hers as well. I know people, mostly men, who have hobbies that do not include their wives. In some, perhaps most, it is because the wife doesn't understand why he likes to do these things. In other cases, it appears that the husband is working to exclude the wife from these activities. Donna has been asked many times if she goes to car events because of me or if she really enjoys them. The truth is that she has come to enjoy them.

I have a friend from high school who posts pictures on Facebook of herself with her guy hunting and fishing. She always has the biggest smile on her face. It warms my heart to see them enjoying life together.

Wives, get interested in what interests your husband even if you don't "get it." Husbands, do likewise. Forsaking takes on a whole new meaning if your hobby creates a wedge. Wives, forcing your husband to give up something because you don't understand it is also a form of forsaking him— as is shutting him out from the things you enjoy. Likewise, husbands, excluding your wife from your hobby or ignoring her interests is also forsaking her.

There is also another side to this. Donna will rarely ask to do something she wants to do as she feels like a burden. I have learned (but only recently) that this makes it my job to figure those things out. Our recent trip to the Monterey Bay Aquarium is a good example of that. We have an upcoming trip to Hearst Castle for many of the same reasons. If I'm not listening to Donna or actively engaging her, I am forsaking her.

Donna had a few things to say about this subject, "Wives, or even husbands, may not voice their desires because of past comments by their spouse or others or a lack of self-worth. One can have a separate interest than their spouse, but still include them. I like to bake and Jim can eat the results. I get the pleasure of riding in a beautiful car and see Jim's accomplishments and hard work."

The more I reflect on these things the more I know how much I have failed to love Donna in this way over the last 40 years. These last two chapters are certainly not the only ways that Jesus loves the church and how we should love our spouse. These are just the ones that He brought to my mind. Look at other ways and apply those in your life as well. Write them down and share them with those around you.

CHAPTER 5
LOVING OUR NEIGHBOR

I know that my wife is my closest neighbor, but who else is my neighbor? The people who live near me? Others? How am I supposed to treat my neighbor? This chapter was very uncomfortable for me to write. I've failed at this so many more times than I have succeeded, but this is the only conclusion I can draw from the words of wisdom found in Luke 10:

> "25 On one occasion an expert in the law stood up to test Jesus. 'Teacher,' he asked, 'what must I do to inherit eternal life?'
> 26 'What is written in the Law?' he replied. 'How do you read it?'

[27] He answered, 'Love the Lord your God with all your heart and with all your soul and with all your strength and with all your mind' and, 'Love your neighbor as yourself.'

[28] 'You have answered correctly,' Jesus replied. 'Do this and you will live.'

[29] But he wanted to justify himself, so he asked Jesus, 'And who is my neighbor?

[30] In reply Jesus said: "A man was going down from Jerusalem to Jericho, when he was attacked by robbers. They stripped him of his clothes, beat him and went away, leaving him half dead. [31] A priest happened to be going down the same road, and when he saw the man, he passed by on the other side. [32] So too, a Levite, when he came to the place and saw him, passed by on the other side. [33] But a Samaritan, as he traveled, came where the man was; and when he saw him, he took pity on him. [34] He went to him and bandaged his wounds, pouring on oil and wine. Then he put the man on his own donkey, brought him to an inn and took care of him. [35] The next day he took out two denarii and gave them to the innkeeper. 'Look after him,' he said, 'and when I return, I will reimburse you for any extra expense you may have.'"

[36] 'Which of these three do you think was a neighbor to the man who fell into the hands of robbers?'

> [37] The expert in the law replied, 'The one
> who had mercy on him.'
> Jesus told him, 'Go and do likewise.'"

Fred Rogers famously asked anybody and everybody if they would be his neighbor, but who is our neighbor, really? The parable of the good Samaritan then establishes that everybody was already Mr. Rogers' neighbor and mine, too. We are to love our neighbor as ourselves, but we need to understand what that looks like. It's not just a nice slogan to put on a wall decoration.

In John 13 Jesus makes this command even more forcefully:

> "[34] A new command I give you: Love one
> another. As I have loved you, so you must
> love one another. [35] By this everyone will
> know that you are my disciples, if you
> love one another."

Love is action, not an emotion. The Bible can tell us a lot about love. We need to dive into what love really is.

In this chapter we will do a deeper dive into 1 Corinthians 13. This is another passage that I have heard many times over the course of my life, but I had never given the words a great deal of thought until now.

> "[4] Love is patient, love is kind. It does not
> envy, it does not boast, it is not proud.
> [5] It does not dishonor others, it is not
> self-seeking, it is not easily angered, it
> keeps no record of wrongs. [6] Love does

not delight in evil but rejoices with the truth. [7] It always protects, always trusts, always hopes, always perseveres. [8] Love never fails..."

Let us now deal with each "Love is" statement separately. With each one look at where you succeed and where you fail.

Patient

The Britannica dictionary puts being patient in the proper light, "...able to remain calm and not become annoyed when waiting for a long time or when dealing with problems or difficult people." I've been known to get annoyed with any sort of delay. I get in the line at the grocery store and am annoyed that there are people in front of me. I just want to get my stuff and get out. It's not their fault that they got there before me. My patience tends to run thin when driving like most people. People tailgating, changing lanes dangerously, running red lights. Yes, those are all bad things, but I can still learn to be patient with them. When Donna wound up needing the wheelchair to get around, I had to become more patient. We can't be patient if we are being selfish.

When my younger son was in the 7th grade, he was taking Algebra. Now, math is one of my strong suits and it is also one of his as he went on to get a degree in math. However, at this point he was struggling because he had spent part of the 6th grade on home studies due to a health problem and missed some of the math instruction. One night while he was trying to do his homework, I was trying to teach him. He started to get mad at me because he didn't understand my words. In a moment of clarity (we all have those from time to time), rather than getting mad in return, I told him to stop. I explained to him that if he didn't understand my words I needed to use different words and it didn't help for him to get mad at me for it. I had been patient with him and that explanation worked as he now knew that he could tell me that he needed different words to understand. This was such a practical, obvious way that patient love showed both of us a better way.

Think about how patient God is with you. When you have trouble with patience remember God's promise to Moses and how long it took for the Israelites to enter the promised land. It took the death of Moses 40 years after leaving Egypt for Joshua to take the Lord's people home.

Joshua 1:

> "5 ...As I was with Moses, so I will be with you; I will never leave you nor forsake you. 6 Be strong and courageous, because you will lead these people to inherit the land I swore to their ancestors to give them."

Proverbs 14: 29 says, "Whoever is patient has great understanding, but one who is quick-tempered displays folly." As we are patient we can understand. When my son was learning Algebra, I would not have been able to understand why he was struggling if I had not been patient. Instead, I would have said something negative and just walked away

I also believe that there is a reason that patience is first in the list. Without patience we will have a very difficult time being kind.

Kind

A Google search on the word, kindness, reveals that the world reveres kindness. There are random acts of kindness that are promoted by people from all beliefs. We can talk about kindness, but we need to know what kindness is. It is giving of oneself without regard to repayment. It is considering others' needs. Think about all the ways that you can be kind to those around you.

Kindness is often found in little things. Letting that person behind you in line at the store with one thing go ahead of you or buying the order of another at the coffee shop are common examples, but let's look at some ways we can show kindness to those we see every day.

At work, it could be lending a hand when it is outside your job duties. While I was working as an electronics technician, there were times I would see a carpenter working by himself when the job really required two people to be done safely. I would stop what I was doing to see if they wanted a hand. The "not my job" attitude prevents kindness in the workplace.

We had a blow-out on one of our cars a few years ago. We had bought a used 2004 BMW 330ci convertible in 2015. The tires were in great shape, but were no match for the massive pothole on Highway 49 between Auburn and Placerville, CA. I pulled off to the side of the road in the tiny town of Cool, CA. We had not had this car for a long time and found that we did not have a lug wrench. I went into a convenience store to ask around about a lug wrench. A young lady who was there in her Jeep offered to loan us a wrench. I got the spare on after trying to figure out the engineering marvel that is a BMW jack (anybody who has ever seen one knows what I am talking about) and thanked her for the wrench. Donna also had a nice conversation with her about life and God. Kindness all around that day.

At home, kindness should be easy, but it can be very hard. After an argument, kindness may very well be the best way to calm things down. This is also the hardest time. It's also hard to be kind when you're feeling selfish. Fix your spouse's favorite meal, go out for ice cream, etc. Look for ways to be kind and you will find them.

Does Not Envy

I have an old friend who can afford to travel wherever she and her husband want to go. When I have seen pictures from their travels I am thrilled. These are places that I cannot afford to go to and I truly enjoy seeing my friends enjoying themselves. At this very moment I have two women I know who are separately visiting Ireland. The pictures on Facebook are great to see if you avoid envy. I have a saying that I travel vicariously through my friends who can afford it. I want to see the pictures of the places they go, whether it's halfway around the world or to the neighborhood park. Be happy for others. Celebrate with them. While there may be competition in this world, don't let winning or losing be the criteria for love.

This is also where sibling rivalries come up and can destroy what is supposed to be a lifelong friendship. Perhaps one sibling is less socially awkward, gets better grades, is a better athlete, or seems to the favored sibling. Envy is the natural outcome, but as adults it can be overcome.

Envy has a different look in the home. The stay-at-home mom can find herself envious of her husband because he gets out of the house every day to go to work. The husband, on the other hand, doesn't understand this because work can just be a chore that has to be done. If both husband and wife work outside the home, one will generally have more success at work than the other. With this, envy can easily follow. How do we work to keep envy at bay? Start with being patient and kind. Join in the joy of success, be a part of it.

As we work on celebrating others' successes our envy will diminish.

Does Not Boast

This is the opposite of envy. This is the attempt to get others to envy you. Facebook is loaded with boasting. Most people don't put their struggles out for all to see, but they do post their victories. While there is nothing wrong with letting others know when good things happen, there is a way to do this that is boasting and another that is rejoicing. I do know that when some people post pictures of their travels, they are met with people who complain and accuse them of being uncaring or flaunting their wealth. If we can recognize our own tendencies to envy and to boast, we can learn to give others grace.

Boasting in a marriage can be devastating to our spouse because it often comes across as stating that you think you are better than they are. At times, I can find myself boasting about my past accomplishments and I know how this can hurt Donna because she thinks more in terms of what she thinks are her failures. I find myself pointing out what she has to boast about, even if she isn't one to boast.

Donna had better grades than I did in school, in part due to her working harder at it, but she is also very smart and has skills that I do not have. There are times I need to remind her of the fact that she took on the challenge and typed over 100 words per minute in high school and of her other accomplishments, one of which was earning the Bank of America award her senior year in business. And, to top that off, even during her darkest years she managed to get our sons to school, help with homework, and try to be a good wife to me.

She thinks of herself as forgettable, but she is far from it. We have a friend we see once or twice a year at car shows. We've been friends for over 40 years. We love him like family. If I see him at a show without Donna the first thing I do is get a hug from him. The second thing that happens is he asks where Donna is. Donna means as much to him, as I do. I have to be patient with her as I remind her.

Is Not Proud

Google (from Oxford Languages) has two definitions of proud. The first one is not what I think Paul is talking about. That is, "...feeling deep pleasure or satisfaction as a result of one's own achievements, qualities, or possessions or those of someone with whom one is closely associated." It is fine to be proud of your children or spouse, proud of your friends. We should also thank God for giving us these people.

On the other hand, and the second definition, is the caution here: "Having or showing a high or excessively high opinion of oneself or one's importance. A proud, arrogant man."

There are so many examples of the pride that Paul is talking about here. I was once accused by a director of the department I was working in of judging people by their intellect. I was able to remain professional, but realized that this was the way he saw me and it would hurt my chances for promotion. The accusation really surprised me because I don't think that way. I think more in terms of what people bring to the table with their own set of skills that will compliment mine. If I need a great ditch digger, I certainly am not going to look at his academic credentials even though they might be great. I was one of the top math and science students in my high school class, but there was one guy who humbled the rest of us. We also thought highly of him, not due to his intellect, but because we genuinely liked him.

I told the manager who accused me of judging others by their intellect that it was a lot like trying to build the fastest car in town. Somebody *will* come along and humble you. It's going to happen so it's good to start out humble and stay that way. I have been around plenty of people who humbled me in so many different ways. There is always a lesson in being humbled. It allows me to see what others have to offer. I have to caution here that being humbled is not the same as being shamed. Shame comes from being found to be something you are not. Humility comes from understanding there are others with greater skills or intellect.

I met a friend fresh out of MIT in the late 1980s. In jest, I describe him as somebody you would be obligated to hate if he weren't such a nice guy. Tall, good looking, and very athletic (in softball he played shortstop and made me look like a very good first baseman as every throw was right at my chest). He was also, obviously, very smart to be able to get into and out of MIT. But as I said, he is also a nice guy. We still have contact through Facebook. He's a CEO today and I love to see what his company is producing (MRI post processing software) and watching as his kids play competitive sports. If I felt like I had to be the smartest guy in the room, I could not have this friendship.

At home, pride can be devastating to your spouse. It is especially difficult if your spouse has a low self-esteem problem. In the short term, you may be getting what you think you want by being seemingly more important than your spouse, but the chasm that divides the two of you will grow larger and larger until it is nearly impossible to close.

Consider 1 Thessalonians 5:

"¹⁰ He died for us so that, whether we are awake or asleep, we may live together with him. ¹¹ Therefore encourage one another and build each other up, just as in fact you are doing."

Build your spouse and others up instead of using your pride to tear them down. Praise them for their accomplishments. Thank them for the things they do. I am learning to thank Donna for doing things she normally does, like laundry. I point out where she has made a positive impact in the lives of others, including myself. When I fix Donna's dinner (most nights), she always thanks me. It's about appreciating the contributions of others.

Does Not Dishonor Others

According to the Collins English dictionary, if you dishonor someone, you behave in a way that damages their good reputation. Consider what you say and how you say it. Gossip is one the most common ways to dishonor someone. The Bible cautions against gossip in several verses, including Proverbs 11:

"¹³ A gossip betrays a confidence, but a trustworthy person keeps a secret."

Paul seemed to still be wary of the Corinthians' resolve to follow the words of 1 Corinthians 13 because in 2 Corinthians 12:20 he wrote:

"For I am afraid that when I come I may not find you as I want you to be, and you may not find me as you want me to be. I fear that there may be discord, jealousy, fits of rage, selfish ambition, slander, gossip, arrogance and disorder."

The ways you can dishonor your spouse are numerous and an entire book could be written about it and probably has been. The most obvious and, perhaps, common way is to make fun of and put down your spouse in front of others. This is especially true if they are there. It seems most sit-coms on television are based on the idea that it is funny to dishonor a spouse with All in the Family among the worst. Archie telling his wife to "stifle it" and calling his son-in-law "Meathead" is the kind of disrespect that dishonors others. Rodney Dangerfield made a living out of disrespect, both toward himself and others, mainly his wife. People laughed, but sadly many also imitated him in their own marriages. We need to be careful how much we emulate popular culture and entertainment. How I speak to and about my wife shows whether I am respecting or disrespecting her.

Much of what I have written in this book about me and about Donna could be written in a dishonoring way. Talk of her depression and her feelings of inadequacy could be construed this way, but I am so proud of her for continuing to fight through these things and for staying with me through my past indifference. Both wives and husbands need to know that the other has their back.

This also holds true for how we speak to our children. Do we praise them for their effort or berate them for lack of achievement? When our sons first started getting grades in school, we told them that we didn't care what grade they got, but expected them to put effort into school. That works with any level of ability, but it also requires paying attention to their effort. When they started driving, we didn't have a set curfew for them. Instead, every time they went out, we had a discussion about where they were going and what time we should expect them to leave. Not only was this showing our teenagers respect, it allowed us to talk about where they were going. Some of this was before cell phones, but if they were going to be late, they showed us enough respect to call us. This wasn't confrontational because it was rooted in mutual respect.

Is Not Self-Seeking

Merriam-Webster defines self-seeking in two ways, "...the act or practice of selfishly advancing one's own ends" and "...seeking only to further one's own interests." There isn't anything wrong with working to achieve success, but when we do that at the expense of others we have entered into the realm of self-seeking. I tended to lack ambition, in part, due to misunderstanding that self-seeking is different than having ambition. Good ambition aims to raise others along with ourselves.

Philippians 2:

> "4 Look out for one another's interests,
> not just for your own."

This doesn't mean to not look out for yourself, but also to look out for others.

The website Divorce.com lists the thirteen most common reasons for divorce. Among the thirteen are; too much conflict, infidelity, domestic violence, addiction, and lack of shared interests. These five are classic examples of being self-seeking.

If there is too much conflict, there is certainly too much self-seeking going on. When you are willing to understand the point of view of your spouse you are less likely to continue arguing. Domestic violence just takes this several steps farther.

Infidelity and addiction are completely self-seeking. They are a pursuit of gratification without regard to your spouse. While addiction may need professional help to overcome it will be worth it in the end.

I have already mentioned getting involved in your spouse's hobbies. If the hobby is something that already appeals to you this isn't very difficult, but if you don't understand the attraction, work at it. Go and enjoy the time with him or her even if the activity isn't something you would choose for yourself.

Donna has a tendency to take not self-seeking too far. She thinks that she is selfish so she won't ask for much as she thinks that she isn't deserving. We have talked about this and are still working toward her feeling less selfish. The truth is that she really isn't selfish.

The more you find yourself putting your selfishness aside the more harmonious your home will be. You will also get more of what you want, but that should never be the motivation or your spouse will start to recognize the pattern. Servanthood fits into this well. As we serve, we start to lose that selfishness that so easily overcomes us.

Is Not Easily Angered

Several places in the Bible, God is referred to as being angered. The key term here is, "easily." Do I get easily angered if somebody cuts me off in traffic because they didn't see me, or DID see me? Do I get easily angered if my neighbor parks "wrong"? Do I get easily angered if the sports team I am rooting for loses a game? It took a long time for God to get angered at His people. We should strive to be a little more like Him.

At home, this takes on a special meaning. There are those who get angry at just about anything. Their spouse will become nervous about saying or doing anything, which brings out more anger. There are those who only feel safe expressing their anger at home, but it is not right for the spouse to endure the sole focus of that anger. Generally speaking, your spouse is not deliberately trying to make you angry (yes, there are those who are broken to the point where this is the behavior that they exhibit). The less you are quick to anger the better your communication will be.

As I reflect on our 40 years of marriage, I think about something I once heard. Look at your spouse's character. Consider any incident in light of who you know them to be. Often awkward comments are not meant to be hurtful and, if considered against the whole, will allow one to take the time to understand rather than jumping right to anger.

Anger also tends to prevent us from being able to listen. As I began to listen to Donna, I started to understand a little. We have been able to work through Donna becoming suicidal again rather than fighting through it. I no longer think, "Here we go again." I think about how I can help. Not getting angry allows me to do this.

Keeps No Record of Wrongs

Oh, this is huge. How many of us still hold on to the wrong that was done to us when we were 8 years old? There may be issues if somebody keeps doing the same thing that they know you see as wrong, but you are still not to keep a record. Some wrongs are severe enough to break a relationship, but keeping a record will only hurt you. It might help if you start keeping a record of "rights", things that people have done for you.

It is especially hurtful if your children think that all you see are their mistakes. They will likely carry that for their entire lives. If they hear the phrase, "You always make that mistake..." or "You'll never get the hang of that..." they will come to believe it. We need to help them grow by working on their shortcomings, but we should make a conscious effort to point out progress and things they do right.

How much more does it hurt your relationship with your spouse if you constantly point out their mistakes. As Donna came to realize that I considered the good times with her to so far outweigh the bad, she began to believe it. She's still not fully there, but with God's help she's getting better.

The more Donna recognizes that I don't bring up the past to shame her the more she sees that I don't keep score. I don't bring up times where she thinks she failed, but I do bring up times where she succeeded or made an impact. Years ago, I was coaching our younger son's youth baseball team (11- and 12-year-olds). We had a great team of baseball players, but some of them had their own problems. While I was coaching their baseball skills, Donna was labeled the team psychologist. She helped those boys see the positive better. There are times that I have to remind her of the impact she had on them. I make a conscious effort to remind her of her impact on others, including on me.

Does Not Delight in Evil

Evil can be described as simply morally wrong. While we all will do things that are morally wrong, it should never delight us. We may say that we never delight in evil, but we may find delight in other's misfortunes.

Remember the story at the end of Chapter 2, the ex-wife 32 years later happy that her ex-husband was dying because he deserved it. How much better would it have been to say nothing? Continuing the fight for that many years kept her from finding enjoyment in life.

Many football fans dislike Tom Brady, which within the context of team sports and having a favorite team is common in this country. However, the delight that some exhibited when his wife left him last year fits this category well. There are so many stories of celebrities' misfortunes and setbacks, but we should never delight in them. We should always remember that they are our neighbor, too.

In marriage, this can be especially detrimental. If Donna is disrespected by anybody, I need to show her that I am on her side. That doesn't necessarily mean that I need to confront that individual, which could make the situation worse. It does mean that I need to listen to her and not belittle her reaction.

Rejoices with the Truth

Truth has made a lot of headlines in recent years. People think they have their "own truth". Merriam-Webster defines truth as, "...the body of real things, events, and facts: ACTUALITY." Truth is not subject to our feelings. It is absolute and we should experience joy with it.

Ephesians 4 describes modern society well: "[14] Then we will no longer be infants, tossed back and forth by the waves, and blown here and there by every wind of teaching and by the cunning and craftiness of people in their deceitful scheming. [15] Instead, speaking the truth in love, we will grow to become in every respect the mature body of him who is the head, that is, Christ." Today we are bombarded with statements that do not hold up to the truth. We need to rejoice in the truth, but we also need to state that truth in love.

This can be a difficult task and will look different with different people. Close friends can hear tough things better than an acquaintance, but often in a marriage you need to say things in a different manner than you would to your friends.

Often, however, truth can be painful. Look back at the list of five common reasons for divorce in the section on love not being self-seeking. If one is involved in any of those things, they are true, but likely hidden from the spouse or others. But we are to rejoice with the truth and there doesn't seem to be any joy in those things. There is usually an indication that one of those things is going on. Joy comes in knowing the truth and being able to confront it with love.

Protects

Google (from Oxford Languages) defines protect as, "...keep safe from harm or injury." This includes physical and emotional harm. It also means to save one from evil.

Ask yourself if you protect those around you, including your spouse, children, and friends.

I worked with a guy who I also considered a friend. He had been conditioned by things in his past to call himself a "dumb Mexican". I took offense to that and told him that, while I had no problem with him calling himself a Mexican, I would not tolerate him calling himself dumb. It took a couple of times telling him to get him to stop, at least in front of me. I had a conversation with his son some time back and mentioned this to him. It bothers him when his dad says these things, but doesn't think he can call him out on it. But he was glad that I did. I don't think my friend ever stopped feeling this way, but he knew I had his back.

Donna has had many of the same feelings about her intellect and about herself in general. If I am to protect her, I need to disagree in the strongest way possible without attacking or belittling her feelings. It is common for me to point out how smart she is. I need to be a safe place for her to tell me when she feels depressed or hurt by others.

Hopes

Look for the best in everyone. This may be difficult with some people that we encounter. With your spouse you need to try to always hope for things to get better than they are, even if things are good already.

Hopes and dreams are hard for Donna to come by so I have to do that for both of us. As we are in our retirement years, we have already reached the hope of not having to work, of being able to spend time with each other.

I have wanted to take a motor home trip around the country for years. Donna worries about affording it while I am hopeful that we will be able to make this a reality within the next couple of years. We are working toward that goal. Within this trip is the desire to see many people, to have the blessing of friendship add to the trip. In 2 and 3 John, he writes at the conclusion of each book of the hope to see the recipients of these two letters in person.

Hope also impacts what we pray for. My hope is that Donna will one day feel the peace of Jesus. Her depression and health problems have made that difficult. I would love for her to find her health again, but peace is more important.

Always Trusts

This isn't so hard with those who have never wronged us, but along with hope, trust that others will do the right thing. Trust that the future is hopeful. Trust that God will work in their lives. Praying for them will help you to have hope and trust.

We put our trust in things every day. We trust that when we turn a light switch on, there will be light. We trust that when we turn the shower on, we will get clean water and that it will be the temperature that we want. We trust that our car will start, move, and stop when we want it to. People, on the other hand, don't always do what we want or expect. Then again, neither do things. That's why we have electricians, plumbers, and mechanics.

Putting trust in people can be a step of faith, especially when someone has been hurt many times by others. When a spouse has done something that will cause the other to lose trust, it can be difficult to get that trust back. However, this tells us to always trust. This is not popular these days. I have heard people say that they will only let another hurt them once and they are done. That's not a good way to approach marriage as two people living together will do things to hurt the trust of the other. Often the same thing repeatedly. There is a saying, "Hurt people, hurt people." Since we are all hurt in one way or another you can see the dilemma. I find that trust comes in realizing the nature of Donna's brokenness and knowing that she is not doing it to me. I can trust that she doesn't want to hurt me.

Perseveres

This goes along with hopes and trusts. Google (from Oxford Languages) defines persevere as, "...continue in a course of action even in the face of difficulty or with little or no prospect of success." We may never get all that we hope for from those we interact with, but we must persevere. I have seen both of my sons and my wife persevere in the face of difficult times. It made me want to persevere with them.

I found out something about perseverance when my older son was in the 7th grade. He wanted to play football. Donna asked the question that every mother does, "What if he gets hurt?" I told her we would deal with it if it happens. Well, it did happen. The first week in pads he broke his arm. The doctor gave us a timeline of when he could resume physical activity. He sat there going over the number of weeks in his head knowing that if he got a week in pads he could play in a game. That game just happened to be the last game of the season. While the doctor advised against it, Alan knew that he could.

We were offered our money back, but Alan didn't want that because he felt that he would no longer be part of the team. From that day to the end of the season he missed two practices, one to go to the library for a school project due the next day and the other for an end of summer church youth group pool party. During that time, he did every part of the workout he could with one arm and he did play in that last game. I would never wish an injury on my children, but I found out what he was made of. He had a great capacity to persevere while we persevered with him.

Jeff had more injuries growing up and through into adulthood, but the one that really stands out occurred in the fall of his junior year of high school. He had transferred schools and was pitching really well in the fall baseball season. Then a freak accident happened. He was playing first base and went across the baseline to catch a throw. The runner came through and their knees collided. Jeff told me how it happened and how it hurt. I knew right then that he had broken his kneecap. The radiologist, however, didn't see it so Jeff pitched the next two weeks on it and did well as it only hurt to run. Donna finally took him to a doctor who read the x-ray correctly. They put him in a knee brace. When Jeff was ready to come back, we all rushed him a little too much and he wasn't ready. This caused him to almost forget how to throw. He had no idea where even a soft toss was going. His coach and I worked with him patiently and finally by the end of the season he was back to his old form. He could have walked away at that point, but he wasn't ready. That perseverance carried him through junior college ball.

Donna's health and depression battles have shown her ability to persevere in the wake of not wanting to. She has fought to get better even when there are setbacks. She gets tired of the fight. She has taught me to persevere with her. If we love, we persevere through all adversity.

Never Fails

God's love never fails, but ours does all the time. If we are to love the way Christ loves, then we should work at failing less often. It can be found in the other "love is" statements of this passage. When we find ourselves more patient and kinder, less envious and boastful, forgetting to count wrongs, less self-seeking and angry we will find that our love will fail less often. Only Christ can reduce my selfishness and help me to love in this manner. Allow Him to reveal these things to you and how you need to change.

Now, remember what the expert's answer was. He said, "Love your neighbor as yourself." Love your neighbor AS YOURSELF. That means we are also supposed to love ourselves in this same way. Read the list of what love is a second time, but this time put yourself in the position of receiving that kind of love from yourself. This will likely be much more uncomfortable than the idea of loving your neighbor in this way, but is, perhaps, more necessary. Now, go back and look a third time and place your spouse into each statement.

I find that the more I think about each "love is" or "love is not" statement I am more conscious of how I need to change my thoughts or behavior. It might be necessary to post 1 Corinthians 13:4-8 on your desk at work, your refrigerator, or in your car and read it daily.

This entire book, along with many others, could be summed up with the golden rule, "Do unto others as you would have them do unto you." The problem is that we all tend to be selfish and want things to go our way. The more we allow God to let us see things His way, the closer we can get to considering others before ourselves.

Conclusion

I have failed more times than I care to count (there's that keeping score thing again) and it has taken me a long time to even address my shortcomings. You may be in the same situation with your marriage being more frustrating than fulfilling, but there is hope in Christ. As we work to become more Christ-like in how we relate to our wife or husband, life will get better and there will be less conflict and stress.

I also find that the more I think about this, the more I recognize the changes I need to make. You'll never change your spouse unless you change yourself first and even then, that cannot be your motivation. Get yourself closer to God and life will change.

I recently read Les and Leslie Parrott's book, *Love is....* I find their afterword in this book to be very comforting as they address their own shortcomings and that they had an alternative motive in writing the book. That is that every time they read it, they are reminded of their need to give love like they write about more than they do. We're all broken, but we don't all admit to it often.

There are no guarantees here. Your spouse is a separate person with their own free will. All you can do is love and pray for healing between the two of you. That is how your heart starts to change. It is now up to you.

SUGGESTED READING (BY THOSE WISER THAN MYSELF) AND RESOURCES

Read other books and look for other interpretations of these themes. I am not an avid reader, but I am looking for more to read. Share these works with your spouse. *Cherish* can be found on Right Now Media as a study. *The Love Chapter* is a compilation of sermons given by St. John Chrysostom who was the archbishop of Constantinople.

1. *Cherish,* Gary Thomas
2. *Love is...,* Les and Leslie Parrott
3. *The Love Chapter,* St. John Chrysostom (ca. 347-407)

Resources:

1. Healthy Marriage Coalition. Local marriage ministry in the Fresno area. growyourmarriage.com

2. Dave and Ashley Willis.
   daveandashleywillis.com

3. Simply Sacred with Gary Thomas.
   https://garythomasbooks.substack.com/

4. Dennis and Barbara Rainey, "The Raineys"
   https://www.theraineys.org/

Many churches today have a thriving marriage ministry. Get involved if your church has one. If not, look around your area or start a ministry. If you need more help look into a Christian marriage/family counselor.

Bibliography

"Access Your Bible from Anywhere." BibleGateway. com: A Searchable Online Bible in over 150 Versions and 50 Languages., New International Version, https://www.biblegateway.com/.

Thomas, Gary L. *Cherish*. Zondervan, 2017.

"Causes of Divorce: 13 of the Most Common Reasons." Online Divorce, https://divorce.com/blog/causes-of-divorce/.

https://www.britannica.com/dictionary

Google, Google, https://www.google.com/. (https://languages.oup.com/google-dictionary-en/)

"Dictionary by Merriam-Webster: America's Most-Trusted Online Dictionary." Merriam-Webster, Merriam-Webster, https://www.merriam-webster.com/.

"Collins English Dictionary: Definitions, Translations, Example Sentences and Pronunciations." Collins English Dictionary | Definitions, Translations, Example Sentences and Pronunciations, https://www.collinsdictionary.com/us/dictionary/english.

Review Inquiry

Hey, it's Jim here.

I hope you've enjoyed the book, finding it both useful and fun. I have a favor to ask you.

Would you consider giving it a rating wherever you bought the book? Online book stores are more likely to promote a book when they feel good about its content, and reader reviews are a great barometer for a book's quality.

So please go to the website of wherever you bought the book, search for my name and the book title, and leave a review. If able, perhaps consider adding a picture of you holding the book. That increases the likelihood your review will be accepted!

Many thanks in advance,

Jim Lusk

WILL YOU SHARE THE LOVE?

Get this book for a friend, associate, or family member!

If you have found this book valuable and know others who would find it useful, consider buying them a copy as a gift. Special bulk discounts are available if you would like your whole team or organization to benefit from reading this. Just email jameslusk@your-closest-neighbor.com or visit Your-Closest-Neighbor.com.

WOULD YOU LIKE JIM LUSK TO SPEAK TO YOUR ORGANIZATION?

Book Jim Now!

Jim Lusk accepts a limited number of speaking/coaching/training engagements each year. To learn how you can bring his message to your organization, email jameslusk@your-closest-neighbor.com or visit Your-Closest-Neighbor.com.

ABOUT THE AUTHOR

 Jim Lusk is a devoted Christian with a passion to help other men in their marriages through the guiding power of God's word. After reflecting deeply on his own marital challenges and closely analyzing key Biblical scriptures, Jim uncovered profound insights on how to restore his marriage. He came to understand God's teachings on living and treating others, especially his wife, Donna. Jim grew up and currently resides in the San Joaquin Valley with Donna. He has an older brother and two grown sons and values strong family bonds. Jim's committed to sharing his faith and wisdom to inspire happier, Christ-centered marriages.

Jim can be reached at: Your-Closest-Neighbor.com.